V is for Viking

A Minnesota Alphabet

Written by Kathy-jo Wargin
Illustrated by Karen Latham and Rebecca Latham

Sleeping Bear Press™

2395 South Huron Pkwy., Suite 200
Ann Arbor, MI 48104
www.sleepingbearpress.com

Printed and bound in the United States.

10 9 8

Library of Congress Cataloging-in-Publication Data
Wargin, Kathy-Jo.
V is for Viking : a Minnesota alphabet / written by Kathy-Jo Wargin;
illustrated by Karen Latham and Rebecca Latham.
p. cm.
Summary: The letters of the alphabet are represented by words, set in short
rhymes with additional information, relating to the state of Minnesota.
ISBN-13: 978-1-58536-125-0
1. Minnesota-Juvenile literature. 2. English language-Alphabet-Juvenile
literature. [1. Minnesota. 2. Alphabet.] I. Latham, Karen, ill. II. Latham,
Rebecca, ill. III. Title.
F606.3 .W37 2003
977.6—dc22   2003013211

This book is dedicated, with love, to all my Minnesota friends.

KATHY-JO

✻

For our family, Bonnie and Ted, and our friends with whom
we share our deep love of wildlife and wild places everywhere.

KAREN & REBECCA

A a

A is for Agates
 one billion years old,
each one has layers
 of red, orange, and gold.

The Lake Superior Agate was adopted as Minnesota's official state gemstone in 1969. Recognized by their brilliant colors and intense striped patterns that appear when polished, these stones are mostly comprised of quartz, and their reddish and orange color comes from iron. Lake Superior Agates are some of the oldest stones in the world, perhaps dating back to a billion or more years ago! They can be found throughout Minnesota near riverbeds and lakeshores.

The Bundt® pan revolutionized the way we vision cakes, and was created by H. David Dalquist of Nordic Ware® in 1950. Since that time, more than 40 million Bundt® cake pans have been sold throughout the world. Imagine all those cakes!

The Boundary Waters Canoe Area Wilderness is a beautiful and pristine area of more than one million acres. Mostly comprised of lakes, islands, and untouched wilderness, only non-motorized boats are allowed. It is located in an area of Minnesota called the Arrowhead country and is part of the Superior National Forest.

B **b**

B is for Bundt® pan—
We must always mention,
this round baking pan
       is a famous invention!

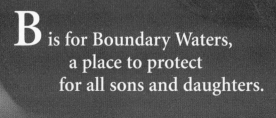

And please don't forget

B is for Boundary Waters,
a place to protect
for all sons and daughters.

C c

Charles Schulz is letter **C**,
he drew the "Peanuts" strip.
And Charles Lindbergh took up flight
in a famous solo trip!

Charles M. Schulz (1922-2000) grew up in St. Paul and was one of the most successful artists and storytellers ever. His cartoon strip "Peanuts" was about a boy named Charlie Brown, his dog Snoopy, and friends Linus, Lucy, Pigpen, and Schroeder. Prior to his "Peanuts" success, Charles Schulz drew a cartoon strip for the *St. Paul Pioneer Press* called "Li'l Folks," which appeared from 1947 to 1950.

Charles Lindbergh (1902-1974) was born in Detroit, Michigan, but grew up on a farm near Little Falls, Minnesota. On May 20-21, 1927, Charles Lindbergh made the first nonstop solo flight across the Atlantic Ocean in his airplane named *The Spirit of St. Louis*.

Now the letter **D** is for Duluth—
its harbor fills with motion
as cargo ships make many trips
both to and from the ocean. Toot! Toot!

Duluth has been an important shipping harbor since the 1880s, when flour was shipped from Duluth to Buffalo, New York. As one of the largest inland seaports in the world, Duluth is part of a common harbor shared by its neighbor city, Superior, Wisconsin. Also known as the Twin Ports, ships navigate the icy waters from late March until mid-January. This shipping port averages approximately 40 million metric tons of cargo per year, making it the largest shipping port on the Great Lakes. Ships travel from Duluth to the ocean via the St. Lawrence Seaway.

Duluth is also home to the Aerial Bridge that lifts to allow large ships and boats to pass.

d
D

Minnesota's first people were Native Americans who lived amidst the lakes, rivers, streams, plains, and prairies of this state. The Ojibwa and Dakota are only two of many Native American cultures that made this area their home. Today, Native American influence can be seen in many ways. Their place names, ideas, and inventions are important to the lives of all Minnesotans; for instance, the word Minnesota is derived from a Dakota word *minisota*, which means sky-tinted waters.

E is for the Early people
and Early Minnesota.
We must not forget the footsteps of
Ojibwa and Dakota.

Ee

Ff

More than one-third of Minnesota is covered in forest, and Minnesotans depend on these vast forests for many reasons. In recent years, state forest industries have harvested more than three million cords of wood fiber annually, almost as much as during the peak of the white pine era in 1900. Forest-based industries such as lumber, wood products, furniture, pulp and papermaking contribute heavily to the economy. However, forest growth and maintenance is important to the health of our woods, and each year, far more trees are planted and grown by natural means than are cut down.

Minnesotans enjoy their forests and many outdoor recreational activities such as camping, hiking, biking, snowshoeing, skiing, hunting, dogsledding, and more.

And Forest starts with letter F,
it gives us many goods.
Paper, pulp, and furniture
are products of our woods.

G g

Minnesota is often referred to as the Gopher State, a nickname resulting from an 1857 satirical cartoon showing nine gophers with the heads of local politicians. They were pulling a locomotive, and satirizing legislative action for a five million dollar railroad proposal. The nickname remained, and later, the University of Minnesota picked it up as well, by naming their mascot, Goldie, the Golden Gopher.

The letter **G** is Gopher
and we think it's really great,
a silly drawing long ago
made us the "Gopher State."

In 1849, Minnesota became a territory with the Missouri and White Earth Rivers forming its western boundary. At that time, Henry Hastings Sibley (1811-1891) was serving as a delegate to the Minnesota Territory. When Minnesota became a state in 1858, he was elected as its first governor. He served from 1858 to 1860. There are many places in Minnesota that are named after Henry Sibley. How many can you name?

H is also for hockey. The United States Hockey Hall of Fame is located in Eveleth. It is a shrine of national importance honoring the legacy of United States ice hockey.

H h

L'ETOILE DU NORD

THE GREAT SEAL OF THE STATE OF MINNESOTA · 1858 ·

H is Henry Hastings Sibley—
it was 1858
when he became the governor
and we became a state.

Itasca State Park is Minnesota's oldest state park. It was established in 1891 to protect the headwaters of the Mississippi River where it begins its 2,552-mile journey to the Gulf of Mexico. Itasca State Park is more than 32,000 acres in size and hosts more than 100 lakes. Here, amidst the pines, you can actually walk across the mighty Mississippi River!

I is for Itasca,
        watch the Mississippi flow,
    as it begins its journey to
            the Gulf of Mexico!

HERE 1475 FT
ABOVE
THE OCEAN
THE MIGHTY
MISSISSIPPI
BEGINS
TO FLOW
ON ITS
WINDING WAY
2552 MILES
TO THE
GULF
OF MEXICO

I i

J j

Now J is Judy Garland,
  she deserves a great applause!
She played the role of Dorothy
  in the film *The Wizard of Oz*.

Judy Garland (1922-1969) was born Frances Ethel Gumm in Grand Rapids, Minnesota. It was in this town that she and her sisters sang and danced at her father's movie house. Eventually her family moved to California, and in 1939 she starred as Dorothy in the film *The Wizard of Oz*. Judy Garland went on to become a well-known singer and actress. You can visit the Judy Garland Museum in Grand Rapids, Minnesota.

k
k
K

The roots of organized softball began when Minneapolis Fire Lt. Louis Rober directed his fire company to play a game that had originated in Chicago. This game, with a "soft" ball and a bat two inches in diameter, flourished when Rober's fire company named themselves the "Kittens," and began to play the game of "Kitten Ball" against other fire companies.

Garrison Keillor, born and raised in Anoka, studied English at the University of Minnesota. In 1974 he launched his variety radio show, *A Prairie Home Companion*, on Minnesota Public Radio. It is based upon life in a fictional Minnesota town called Lake Wobegon, and is heard by approximately 3.9 million United States listeners each week.

The letter **K** is Kitten Ball,
a fun and easy game.
First played to keep the firemen fit,
now softball is its name.

And **K** is Garrison Keillor
with his Minnesota show,
A Prairie Home Companion
is heard on the radio.

Please tune in, it's ready to begin!

L l

L is for Loon,
    watch it float back and forth.
Its beautiful sound
    is our song of the north!

And L is for Lakes,
    we do have a lot.
With more than ten thousand,
    they're easy to spot!

The Common Loon, or *Gavia immer*, is the Minnesota state bird and one of the oldest living species of birds. Loons make nurseries for their young in quiet, shallow lake or pond coves, which are plentiful throughout the state. The common loon is notorious for its three distinct and haunting calls—the wail, the yodel, and the tremolo.

Often referred to as the Land of 10,000 Lakes, there are actually more than 11,000 ten-plus acre lakes in Minnesota. The largest inland lake is Red Lake, which is over 288,000 acres in size. Other large lakes include Mille Lacs, Leech, Winnibigoshish, and Lake Vermilion.

The Mall of America in Bloomington is the nation's largest retail and entertainment complex, boasting more than 520 stores. The mall, which is also known as the "MegaMall" to most Minnesotans, was completed in 1992, and is one of the most visited destinations in the United States, and has more visitors annually than the Grand Canyon, Disney World, and Graceland combined.

m
M

Mall of America begins with **M**,
the place for shopping fun.
The largest in the USA,
a treat for everyone!

N is for North Star
leading us forth—
L'Étoile du Nord
means "The Star of the North."

n

N

Minnesota's official motto is *"L' Étoile du Nord,"* a French saying that means the North Star, so Minnesota is often called the North Star State. The phrase appears on the state seal and other official documents, and was created to acknowledge the North Star, otherwise known as Polaris. This symbol represents the forward reach into the United States, as well as the spirit of the French-speaking explorers who were important to the establishment of Minnesota.

As the star nearest the north, the North Star marks the tail of the Little Dipper, and always reveals the direction north to an observer.

O is for Ore Boat
that waits near the shore,
to fill with the cargo
we call iron ore.

Prospectors and explorers headed for northeastern Minnesota when they heard reports of gold being discovered there. Since that time, iron ore has played an important part in the development of Minnesota, and especially the settling of Minnesota's Iron Range, which is located in a portion of northeastern Minnesota often referred to as the Arrowhead region. Iron ore was first discovered on the Vermilion Iron Range in the mid 1880s, followed by the discovery of iron ore on the nearby Mesabi Iron Range, which was the largest iron ore deposit of the Lake Superior region. By the turn of the century, Minnesota led the nation by producing more iron ore than all other ranges combined. The Iron Range of Minnesota also includes the Cuyuna Range, discovered in the 1890s, which lies east and north of Brainerd.

Oo

P p

The pink and white lady's slipper, or "showy" lady's slipper is the official state flower of Minnesota, and is actually an orchid species that thrives in damp, low-lying areas such as bogs, swamps, and woods. The lady's slipper grows slowly, and may take many years to produce a flower. Also called the moccasin flower because of its shoe-like shape, the lady's slipper is special and rare, and is illegal to pick.

P is Pink and White Lady's Slipper
in the morning dew.
Some call it the moccasin flower
because it's shaped like a shoe.

Winter has always been a time for quilting, the sewing of a special blanket that often tells stories through its colors and patterns. It is a tradition that many ethnic groups and cultures in Minnesota have continued throughout the years. Not so long ago, Minnesota became home to immigrants from European areas such as Scandinavia, Germany, Poland, and Italy, as they came to work in the lumber camps, mines, and shipping industries. Today Minnesota enjoys even greater diversity in its cultures, with the largest concentration of Hmong in the United States, as well as the nation's second largest population of Tibetans.

Q is for the many Quilts
sewn by many hands.
People came to Minnesota
from many distant lands.

Q
q

R r

R is for the Red Pine,
 its bark is reddish-brown—
Its needles grow in sets of two,
 with pinecones for its crown.

And **R** is for the Rivers,
 watch them flowing wild and free.
Minnesota, Red, and Mississippi
 are our biggest three!

The Minnesota state tree is called the Red Pine, or *Pinus resinosa*, due to its reddish-brown bark. It stands approximately 60-100 feet tall when mature, and its long green needles grow in pairs. Often called the Norway Pine, it did not actually come from Norway but was named by early European explorers who thought it was the same type of tree they had seen in Norway.

Minnesota has numerous rivers. The Mississippi, Minnesota, and the Red River are the three largest rivers in the state. These rivers and others have played important roles in the development of agricultural and lumber industries of the past.

Now **S** is for the Sugar Beets.
We do love to boast
that in the whole United States
our farmers grow the most! Sweet treat!

Minnesota leads the nation in the production of sugar beets, producing more than eight million tons of sugar beets per year. These sugar beets are primarily processed into white and brown sugars, and thrive in approximately 25 Minnesota counties, although most of the production is in the Red River Valley area.

Ss

Tt

T is for Twin Cities,
      Minneapolis and St. Paul.
Divided by a river,
      both are loved by all!

Minneapolis and St. Paul are the two largest cities in Minnesota. Affectionately nicknamed the "Twin Cities," they are divided by the Mississippi River. St. Paul is the state capital, and Minneapolis hosts a thriving business, retail, theater, and arts atmosphere, as well as the Hubert H. Humphrey Metrodome.

St. Paul has always been the capital city of Minnesota. There have been three different capitol buildings, with the most recent being built in 1905. It is well-known for its outdoor statue, a gold-leafed copper and steel grouping known as the Quadriga or "Progress of the State." In it there are four horses which represent the power of nature: earth, wind, fire, and water. There are two women who symbolize industry and agriculture, which together symbolize civilization. Lastly, the man standing on top represents prosperity.

St. Paul is the capital,
it's where the laws are made—
Minneapolis has the Metrodome
where many sports are played!

Mississippi River

U is for the Underground Mine,
deep and out of sight.
The miners worked extracting ore
with very little light.

When mining operations at the Tower Soudan Underground Mine ceased in the early 1960s, the mine, which goes 2,400 feet beneath the surface, became Tower Soudan State Park, hosting tours below the ground. Here, visitors can experience the inner workings of an actual underground mine. Over time, it has become the host place for a high-energy physics lab, located at the bottom of the mine, where scientists use its depth to filter out cosmic rays that interfere with sensitive scientific experiments.

At this time, scientists from all over the world, through the University of Minnesota, are trying to measure particles called neutrinos, which are smaller than the nuclei of atoms, in an effort to discover what the universe is made of.

U u

V

V is for the Vikings,
   some believe they came in ships,
and left behind a rune stone
   to tell us of their trips.

Many people believe that Vikings visited the area we now know as Minnesota as early as the fourteenth century. The Kensington Rune Stone, a stone with runic Viking inscription, was found in a field in Minnesota by a farmer named Olof Ohman, and the inscription, once deciphered, was said to tell a tale of a Viking expedition in the year 1362. This stone, however, has proved to be the point of much discussion between those who believe it is valid and those who don't.

Regardless of its authenticity, Viking heritage and Viking lore have made an impact on Minnesota, and can be seen throughout the state, as well as in the name of the professional football team, the Minnesota Vikings.

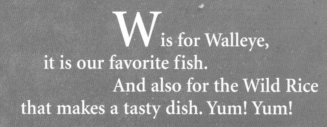

W is for Walleye,
it is our favorite fish.
And also for the Wild Rice
that makes a tasty dish. Yum! Yum!

The Walleye is the state fish of Minnesota. It is a fun fish to catch, and although it lives in all parts of the state, it thrives in the large cool lakes of northern Minnesota.

Wild Rice is an aquatic grass and the only cereal grain that is native to the United States. It is the state grain of Minnesota, and has long been hand-harvested by Native Americans. Also harvested by commercial producers who use specialized machines, Minnesota grows more than six million pounds of wild rice per year.

W
W

Laura Ingalls Wilder wrote children's books such as *Little House on the Prairie*, *Little House in the Big Woods*, *On the Banks of Plum Creek*, and *By the Shores of Silver Lake*. Her book *Little House on the Prairie* was made into a television show portraying the Ingalls family living in Walnut Grove. Laura Ingalls and her family actually lived in a town called Walnut Grove, Minnesota, for a brief time when Laura was a young girl, in a dugout home near the banks of Plum Creek.

X marks the town of Walnut Grove.
Come and take a peek,
where Laura Ingalls Wilder lived
on the Banks of Plum Creek.

Walnut Grove
X

X

x

Yy

And **Y** is for the Yellow fields
rolling in the sun.
Canola, corn, and sunflowers
make oil for everyone.

And don't forget our prairies:
They are beautiful and mellow,
in southern Minnesota
fields of blue and green and yellow.

Oil crops such as yellow-flowered canola, sunflowers, and corn produce oil used for frying and baking. Minnesota is one of the leading producers of oil crops, turning out more than one billion pounds of vegetable oil per year.

When settlers came to Minnesota, a vast, abundant tallgrass prairie existed over much of western and lower Minnesota. These prairies were a complex ecosystem of plants and grasses and included animals such as free-roaming bison and pronghorn antelope. Today, less than 1% of that native prairie remains. Minnesota is dedicated to preserving those remaining remnants, and you can learn about them at sites such as Prairie at Blue Mounds, Kellogg-Weaver Dunes, Hole-in-the-Mountain Preserve near the South Dakota-Minnesota Border, the Ordway Prairie Preserve in west-central Minnesota, and the Bluestem Prairie Preserve near Moorhead, which is designated as a state Scientific and Natural Area.

Minnesota is known for its northern-most position of all the United States. As well, International Falls has earned the title "nation's icebox," not only for its cold weather, but also for its cold weather research laboratory, which tests equipment and products to see how they react to extreme cold temperatures.

Although Minnesota is known for chilly weather, Minnesotans have a long-standing reputation for enjoying outdoor activities such as skiing, snowmobiling, snowshoeing, ice fishing, skating, sledding, and more.

Z is for below Zero.
We are known for chilly places,
but even when it's cold outside
we still wear smiling faces!

In Minnesota, hearts are warm
and friendly as can be,
and you've just learned about it
in Minnesota A to Z!

A Lake-ful of Minnesota Facts

1. What Minnesota state symbol is one of the oldest living birds?

2. Who was the first governor of Minnesota?

3. What kind of game is Kitten Ball?

4. Which Twin City is the capital of Minnesota?

5. What is the only cereal grain that is native to the United States?

6. This state gemstone is comprised mostly of quartz and, when polished, has brilliant colors and striped patterns—What is it called?

7. This famous Minnesotan made the first nonstop solo airplane flight across the Atlantic Ocean—Who was he?

8. What does the word Minnesota mean?

9. Minnesota is often referred to as the Land of 10,000 Lakes. What is the name of its largest inland lake?

10. What is the Minnesota state tree?

11. What are the three largest rivers in Minnesota?

12. Minnesota leads the nation in producing what root vegetable?

13. What ancient relic was found in a Minnesota field and said to be of Viking origin?

14. The author of the beloved *Little House* children's book series lived in Walnut Grove—What is her name?

15. This cartoonist grew up in St. Paul and was made famous by his "Peanut" characters Charlie Brown and Snoopy.

Answers

1. The loon

2. Henry Hastings Sibley

3. Kitten Ball was an early name for organized softball.

4. St. Paul

5. Wild Rice

6. The Lake Superior Agate

7. Charles Lindbergh

8. It is derived from the Dakota word minisota and means sky-tinted waters.

9. At more than 288,000 acres in size, Red Lake is Minnesota's largest inland lake.

10. The Red Pine

11. The Mississippi, Minnesota, and the Red River

12. The sugar beet

13. The Kensington Rune Stone

14. Laura Ingalls Wilder

15. Charles M. Schultz

Kathy-jo Wargin

Author Kathy-jo Wargin has earned national acclaim with award-winning titles such as Michigan's Official Children's Book *The Legend of Sleeping Bear* and Children's Choice Award winner *The Legend of the Loon*, and many others. Her most recent title is *The Edmund Fitzgerald: The Song of the Bell*.

Born in Tower, Minnesota, Kathy-jo (Nelson) lived in Grand Rapids, Minnesota, for most of her life, and studied music-composition at the University of Minnesota-Duluth. With more than 15 books in publication, she is a frequent lecturer and guest speaker throughout the country. She lives in Petoskey, Michigan, with her husband, photographer Ed Wargin, and their son Jake. For more information, you can visit her website at www.edwargin.com.

Karen & Rebecca Latham

Noted wildlife artist Karen Latham has won numerous awards, including Canadian Conservation Stamps for the Yukon Territory (2002), New Brunswick (2003), and Alberta (2003). She also was second runner up in the 2002 Federal Duck Stamp Competition. Daughter Rebecca has followed in her mother's award-winning footsteps with numerous accolades including first runner up in the 1998 Federal Junior Duck Stamp Competition, winner of the 2002 Minnesota Turkey Stamp Competition, and the Canadian Conservation Stamp for Manitoba (2003). Both are signature members of the Society of Animal Artists. The Lathams' studio is in Hastings, Minnesota.